Happy Children

By the Pupils of
THE LONSDALE C. of E. PRIMARY SCHOOL

PRINTED & PUBLISHED BY:
WINE PRESS, 1 SILVER STREET, TAMWORTH
01827 67622

The Lonsdale C. of E. Primary School
July 1996
ISBN 1 899705 68 6   £4.00

The Best Player Ever

I admire one particular person who uses his skills well. He scores brilliant goals. This is Eric Cantona. He takes the ball round people by swerving and out-pacing them and sending them the wrong way. He sets them up by crossing or passing the ball. He plays for Manchester United. He has helped them win the F.A. Cup and the Premiership twice. When I am older I would like to have the skill that he has and score goals like does. That is my ambition.

Name Robert Hodson

Age 11

I WISH........

I wish I was the best Footballer. I wish I was playing for Manchester United. I wish I was the best person on earth. I wish I had all the money. I wish I had all the chocolate I wanted.

John Edwards

Love

Love is the colour of a red red heart smiling a happy smile.
It tastes of a big round chocolate cake that doesn't make sick.
It smells of spices freshly picked or a rose with soft, silky petals.
It sounds like happy, laughing, lively people singing a happy song.
It feels soft and warm like bright golden sunshine or a cushion in your favourite chair.
Some people say love makes the world go round.
Do you think it's true?

by Hayley Bates
age 11

I wish......

I wish I could play for Manchester United and I will wear a red tee-shirt and white shorts.

Robert Robinson

Cowboy Cat

I am a cat which likes to have adventures and play. I chase birds and flies and anything that moves but I am a bit of a twit because I am scared of gerbils. I go all over the place with Brandy, next doors cat. I hate it when I am called in to the house because I might be on an adventure and I don't know the way back to my owner in the dark. My name is Sooty because I am black. I have white feet like boots and a white neck like a handkerchief. Is that why I am adventurous?

Paul Nurrilow
age 11

When I grow up

When I grow up I will be a football player and play for Wolves I will train very hard if I can't be a football player I will join the Army But if I can't do any of those I hope to have a healthy life.

Ricky Arnold 3/4S

I like School

I like School I like namber work and the stories and painting and wordbuilding and play times by Laura Gittins 1J

When I grow up

When I grow up I would like to be a professional footballer and play for Aston Villa. My favourite player is Savo Milosovic. My favourite goal keeper is Mark Bosnich. Mark Bosnich is my favourite goal keeper because he has saved lots of goals.

by William Martin

All about me

When I grow up I want to be a lorry driver. I will take things to supermarkets. I have got a pet cat his name is Charlie when I come back from school ner he runs to the door then he goes with me to the capboerd and I get his food and put in a dish

John Foster age 7

What I like. I like my school because I like playing in polydron.

by Michael W.

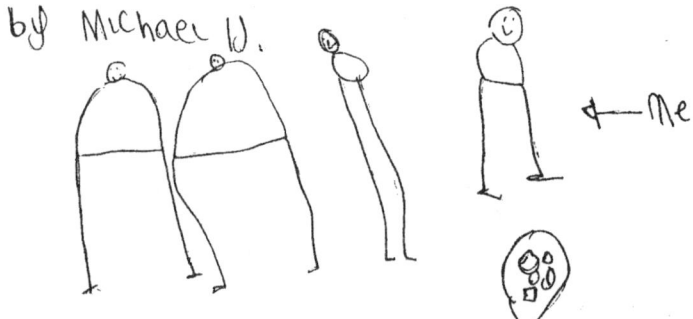

← me

My pet

My pet is a dog. She is brown and white. When I go to bed she barks all night. In the morning she gives me a fright by jumping on my bed. I give her some milk and crawl back to bed.

Katiesord

My school.

I like my school because I like P.E. And I like the teachers they are kind. And I like number work. Most of all I like my friends and my teachers. Hannah Silcox.
IJ

When I grow up

I want to be a policeman when I grow up it will be good fun because I have seen a policeman work I have been in a police station and it was interesting My grandad used to be a policeman

Matthew Redfern

Sea pollution

We have to look after our world if we don't it will be a horrible place. We need to be careful if we don't tankers and other things will sink and spread oil. This affects animals fish and even seagulls. If we don't take any notice the oil will kill every thing in the sea and there will be nothing living in the sea and the world will be a horrible place to live. On news round I saw a dead shark and little dead fishes all around it. There were also dead seagulls.

James Hughes 9

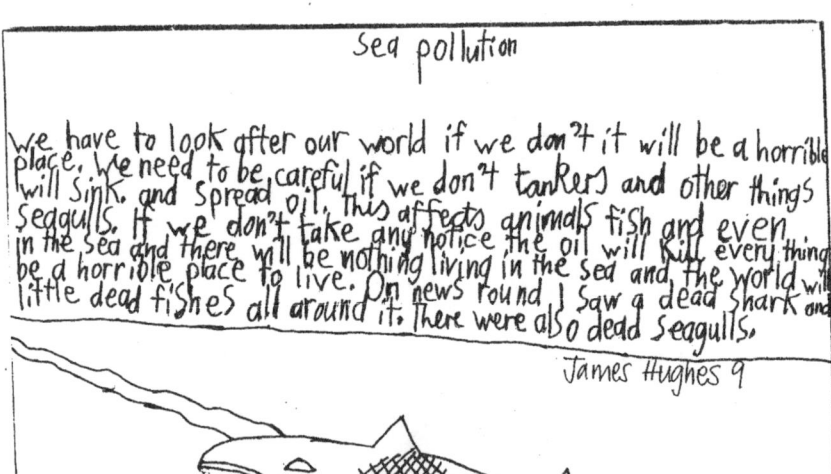

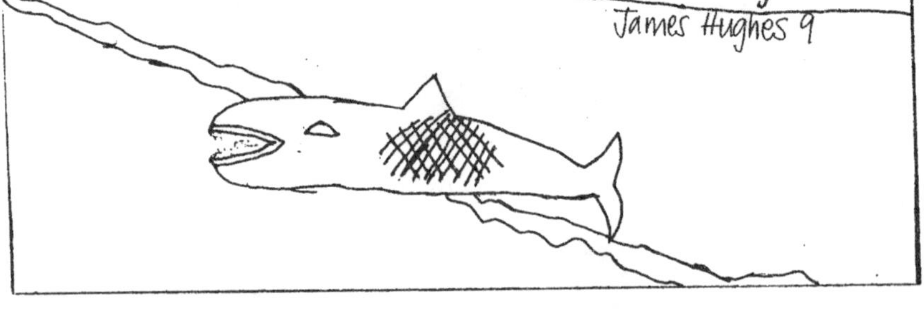

My Extra-Special Day

For my extra-special day I would like to go back in time to meet the dinosaurs and go on an adventure with them. And the dinosaurs would become my friends and I would have a ride on a Diplodocus. And I would go past an exploding volcano. That's what I would like to do on my extra-special day.

Heather Boulton.

The Dustbin

by Sam Foster age 11

He is just around the corner,
Opening his mouth wide.
With a wide green smile,
a big green body and creeky black wheels
Spiders, flies and cobwebs everywhere.
I don't want to do this misson,
It's scary, horrible with spiders and flies attacking you.
I run as fast as I can, clutching my bulging, white plastic bag
He opens his mouth.
Will I ever get back to base safe?
So I throw the plastic bag, it sails through the air and then BANG! SMASH! it is in,
and I run away.
It wasn't really that bad putting rubbish in the dust bin

My Pets

I've got a pet. My pet is called Poppit. Each time we go to bed Poppit climbs onto the bed and he keeps tickling my feet

Kelly Foster 8

I Wish.........

I wish that I could have a dog because then the dog can wake me up in the morning.

Joshua Simkin

The world is good,
The forests are nice
Animals can be good,
Some can be nasty.
Squirrels climb trees
Teachers help with work,
Mums look after you.
Dads they cook for you.
Friends can be kind,
I like the world

Rhiannon Winn 7

I wish......
I wish I could be a vet because I can make animals better.

Victoria Evans.

Mark Roome

I like playing wit
h them obilo at schoe~

ccassrf

I wish ....

I wish I could have an adventure with
my friends. An exiting one with smugglers
and gold, hiding from the smugglers and
getting all the gold, I read Enid Blyton's
Famous five books and I feel like I
am joining in the adventures, I wish I could
have any sort of adventures, if only
I could have one!
  Nicola Wood 8

my friends me

Smugglers
Where's that gold?
Where's that gold?

I Like doing writing at school
David Wallbanks
class SRF

The World

The world is a funny place,
~~horrible,~~
In Africa the people are sick,
~~Horrid,~~
Why is it this way?
Oh! What can we do?
Run away animals
The sea is polluted
Love is no more for you.
Dolphins are dying,
By the minute

Thomas Hughes age 9

When I grow up I want to be a teacher and I will teach the chlidren how to write proplee and play quietly and not to shout at each other

·Sarah Leigh.

Victoria Foxley class RH
I like to play in the sand

Special times

A special time for me was when my Aunty Teressa had a baby Her name was Rebecca, Her fingers were so tiny and her feet were so small. Although she is a cute baby. every time I see her she had grown a bit more.

by miranda Dale Age 10.

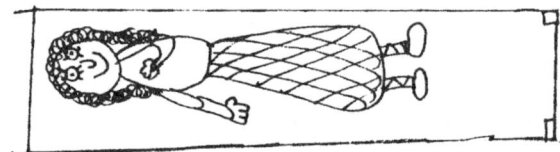

Hannah Telfer.
CLASS RH
I like going swimming

Myself

4 x 2 = ☐

8 ⟌ 253

56
+ 91
―――
1 X 0

I am normally easy going and take life as it comes but if I blow (get angry) I go bright red in the face (like a beetroot). people say I am good at maths but I'm only in the top group like a few people. Maths is my favourite subject because I like numbers. When I grow up I would like to be a policeman because I like the feeling of helping others.
I like the feeling of doing well in everything I do. I like Gina G's music and Caribbean music because its lively.

by Martyn Barry Haskins
Age 10 yrs

When I grow up I wish that I can be a farmer because I can feed the animals. Katy Silcox

When I grow up I would like to be a teacher because I would like to teach children and I can read them a story and if they need a word I would put it in a word book. Allana Clark.

Frances LWkley class RH
I lkes wemmunewut n
my arm bands

Myself

Hi! My name is Damon. My hobbies are cricket and football. I'd rather play football more than cricket. Something that bothers me is when my little baby brother screws my Home Work up. Something special about me is I'm good at science, Maths, Art and english. When I'm alone I like to read sometimes. My favourite place to be is some where with good things. I like friend's who are nice to me. I wish I could have all the stuff of dogs in the world. I feel nervous when I have to talk in front of a big crowd. Better than anything I like to be at my dads.

By Damon aged 9 years old.

Thomas Foxley
Class R

I Like playing on the computer

THE LION.

One day Caroline went for a walk. In a misty dark dusty wood. She heard a whine. She looked behind a bush She saw a lion. It had a thorn in it's paw. She bent down and pulled out the thorn. The lion got up. She stroked the lion and the lion went with her. Then they met a pack of wolves. Caroline was terrified She ran back, until she saw a big tree. She climbed up it so she was safe while the lion chased the wolves away. Then he came back for Caroline.

By Charlotte Leigh.
Age 8

Sophie Wojtulewicz   class RH

I like playing Princesses in the playground

My pirate

My pirate has got long curly orange hair. He has got big dirty black ears. He also has one hairy black eyebrow and the other one is painted black. My pirate has got one green eye and the other one is a green glass eye. My pirate has a big fat runny nose. He has three jagged teeth and spiky hairs comming out of his tongue. My pirate is a fat tall pirate and he wears a big holey tee shirt and dirty patched trowsers. His name is hairy chops.

by Laura Hammond   aged 8

Dahieue
I like at school
down
sitting

Clark
school

Class RF

I wish
I wish there was no pollution
so that everybody could
breath clean air. Bad air
makes me cough
I wish I could go bungee
jumping on holiday
   Alastair Vaughan 8

Luke Edwards
I like playing with the mobilo at school

class RF

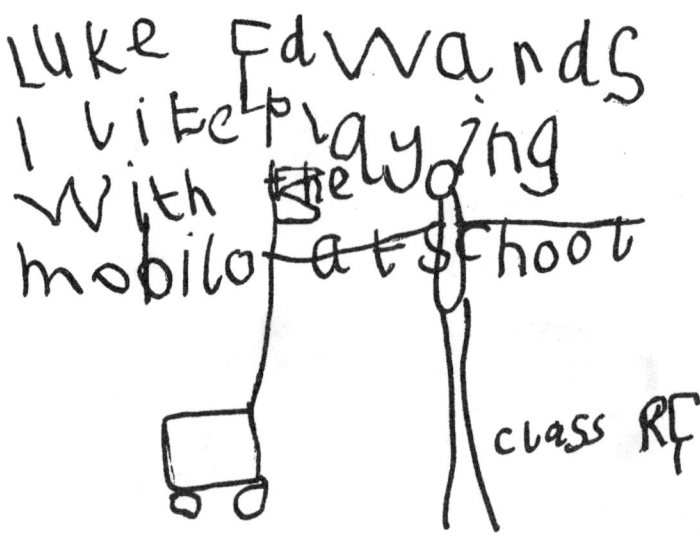

michael wheeler 8   Date 1st may

my fish

I have three fish one called Pepsi another called Orange-
-ade and another called Vimto. This morning Orange ade
banged his nose on the weed they are all funny Sometimes
Vimto is the smallest but eats the most. Pepsi is shaped
Like a shark Vimto is black, white and orange. Orangeade is orange
with a black tail and Pepsi is red and white. We only got them two
weeks ago.

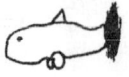

I like playing in the shop at school class of Sophie Parry

We are thinking about plants for our topic this term so I'm writing about plants. They are very important because they give us oxygen. The seeds inside produce new flowers when the old ones die. They grow tiny little roots. A heavy shower will be a nice drink for them the sun makes them open up their petals. Trees shade you when you are hot little leaves or blossom make the trees or plants look beautiful.

by Harry Gardner 8

When I grow up

When I grow up I want to be an Astronaut and go up in a rocket and see the moon and a comet. I could study the planets. It would be fun eating food in mid air because the gravity has gone.

by
Robert Whitfield
age 10½

My name is John Shepherd and I will tell you about myself. My favourite animal is a hamster because I like them. I wish I played football every day. My hobby is football. My pets are guinea pigs and dogs. I had a dog but it died. I like doing maths. I've got two sisters and one brother. When I get older I want to be a farmer because my Dad is a farmer. My special time was when my dog had puppies. I go on holiday once a year. I like the springtime and summer because the butterflies come out. My favourite time of year is Christmas because all my family come over to my house. My parents take me camping once a year. I like swimming. My house has three floors. My Grandma always gives me sweets.

By John

Myself

I have got hazel eyes and brown and blond hair. I am mostly good tempered but sometimes bad tempered. When I get angry I get very angry and take it out on other people. I go to cubs on a Monday and gym on a Thursday. I would like to be a gymnast when I grow up. I have got one brother, two dogs and ten gold fish. I like animals but I dont like birds.

by
Laura Rogers
Age 10

Special Times

My special time was when I went to Disneyland in Paris because I liked the rides and my family was all together. My favourite ride was the run away train, I was too small to go on Space Mountain but my brother and sister said it was very good. We stayed in Disneyland for two days. We were going to watch the fire works but we would have missed the ferry if we did. I had a lovely time and I would love to go again.

By Laura Heelis

Age 10

I Wish

I have always wished to go on the beach with my pony Chester and canter just were the water laps over the sand on a nice hot day when the sun is shining. I have also wished to travel around the world. That is my biggest wish because I would like to see how other people live. I would mostly like to go to America so I can go to Disney land and go on the new ride.

by Katie Jones
Age 10.

Red

Red is a poppy,
Red is a juicy strawberry,
Red is an apple,
Red is a rose,
Red is red paint,
Red juicy grapes,
Red is a tan,
Red cheeks,
Red is a berry.

Leanne Boulton

Age 9   My pirate   John Batten

My pirate has got a curve with points on the top and the hair couler is blackish and a bit of brown. His ears are stenching smelly pongy and crinkly. His eye brows are stinging sharp eye brows! His eye is one giegantic enormese stenching eye and the other is a patch. His nose is a slobbrey snobby nose that pongs. His teeth are yellow rotting revolting stench. hes got stinking smelly food stuck on the discusting moustache. His breath is stinky. His body size is enormese fat tall bolgy. His sord is a riggly sord with a point thats as sharp as a sharks tooth and a hand thats got discusting warts and moles and discusting feet that is rotting and one wooden leg cracked and clothes that are to small and ragged.

Red

Red is a rose.
Red is a colour.
Red is the sun going down.
Red is the blood.
Red is a tulip
Red is a flower.
Red is an apple.

Chloe Foster

apple flower tulip blood sun going down

Space

P is for planets so dull and so bright,
L is for look at the planets you like,
A is for alien that you really hate,
N is for neptune that's got lots of slate,
E is for energy that makes you float around,
T is for thousands that are abound,
S is for saturn that's shining on you,

By Rebecca Timmis
Age 8

Red

Red is for leaves in Autumn,
Red is for a red apple,
Red cherries,
Red rose,
Red berry,
Red lips,
Red tulips,
Redheart.

Emily Platt

All the rainy day are here.
Util the sun comes again.
the leaves are in there colours.
Ugly toads are enjoying the rain.
My trousers are good and warm.
dad picks up the leaves
and I help to.
you and I look at the berries
So the birds can live.

By Laura
Telfer
age 8

Red

Red is fire,

Red is a bus,

Red is a rose,

Red is an apple,

Richard Hopley

Timothy Rawling 7

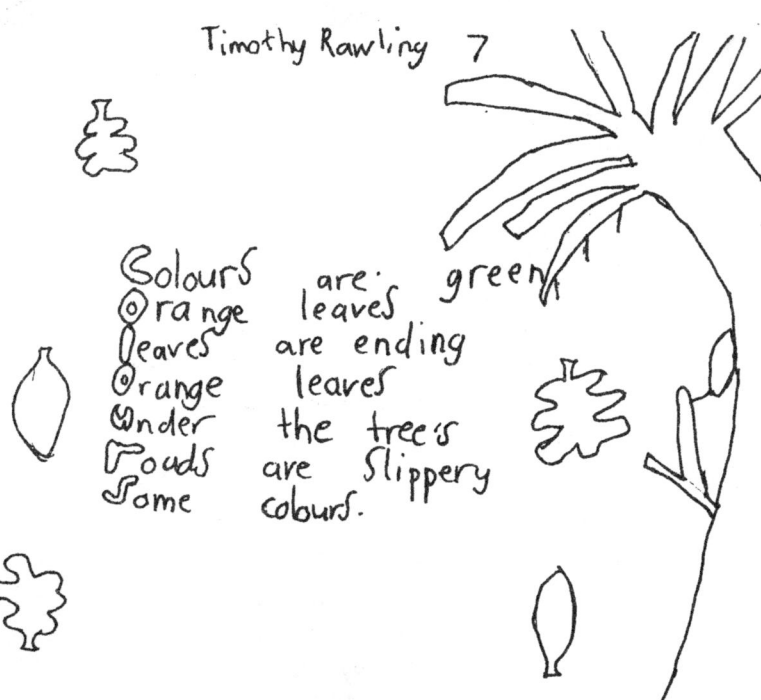

Colours are green
Orange leaves
Leaves are ending
Orange leaves
Under the tree's
Roads are slippery
Some colours.

Green

Green is grass,
Green is a pea,
Green is a frog,
Green is an apple,
Green is a tree.
Shaun Bickley

Golden flames up in the sky,
Flashing magic here and there,
Burning flames up, up high,
Golden stars going round and round,
Different colours here and there,
Glowing stars up, up high,
Burning rocket go up into the sky,
Planets are far from the ground,
Dazzling stars all around.

By Kayleigh
age 9

yellow

yellow is a daffodil,
yellow is a sunshine,
yellow is a sunflower,
yellow is a leaf,
yellow is a banana,
yellow is a school shirt,
yellow is a cheese sandwich.

Charlotte Russell

Mars

Modern space ships,
Amazing twinkling stars,
Red and green flashes,
Stars flashing here and there, Take off

Zoom

Zooming comets,
overhead stars,
over the stars a bright and gleaming sun,
Moons are floating every where,

by Kerry fellows
age nine

Green

The blowing grass in the wind,
The leaves on the trees,
The moss on the wall,
The prikly bush,
The buds on the branches,
The school Jumper.

moss on the wall

Richard Dudley the school Jumper

grass

My pirate

My pirate has got brown dirty hair which is full of dandruff. His ears are scabby and hairy and full of ear wax. His eyes are are sleepy and bloodshotted with a serious look. His eyebrows are full of sleep and very dirty. His nose is snotty and red and pointed. His teeth are yellow and slimy and full of plague and decay. His face has got a big beard with food and spit and debris over his face. He is fat and tall. He wears black and blue rags with swords, he has only one arm and one leg.

His name is
Captain Bloodthirsty

James Kropp
age 9

The Best

Super striker Mike Sheron plays for Stoke City, the best team in the world. I wish I could play left wing for them and score as many goals as the fantastic Mike. He moved to this excellent team in December this year. He used to be at Norwich. He came to Stoke in a swap deal with Keith Scott. (Hurrah). He is 27 years old. Mike has lifted Stoke to the play-offs with fifteen glorious goals since his move and nearly got them into the premiership because of all these magnificent efforts. He should be playing centre forward for England but instead he plays for me - in my team - the best team - since football began.

by James Shelley Age 11

Horror Hamsters

I used to have two hamsters,
They got it into their heads,
That every time
They're out of their cage,
They can jump up on my bed!
And when at night I'm sleeping,
And there's not a sound at all,
You'll hear squeaks, thumps and scratching.
As they both escape, scurry away.
Out through my bedroom door and down into the hall.
Now my two horror hamsters,
Who used to climb upon my bed,
Went too far, they thought they'd try my mothers nice warm bed.
They escaped at night, give my mum a fright.
And now of course, they're dead.

Jenny Stuart age 11.

Book Fair, By Ben Wardle aged 11

Books are adventurous clever and fine.
Open a book and there you will find.
a picture in the middle, that stays in your mind.

Orange and blue, yellow and green,
some books are nice and some books are mean.
Kings of the books jump out at night,
they give you adventures and say sleep tight.
Far far away are the lost books of the land,
they play a song from the musitions hand.
A lot of books are in your dreams,
some make you excited, and some make you scream
Invented stories stay in your mind, black and white
with good designs.
Remember the stories you have read, keep them inside
your brainy head.

The Chipmunks Escape

"There, there," I said. "Under the sette." "It's no use," Kelly said. "He's to fast." "I've got him" I said. "Ouch!" "He bit me." After half an hour of trying to get the Chipmunk back again, it was just the same.
"There he goes." "Where, where?" "Up the stairs." "Come on." But as soon as we got there Sonic (the Chipmunk) came down with the hampster food.
"I've got an idea," I said. I got a bag of hampster food and lead then into the cage. Sonic wasn't very lucky and got caught in the cage. Got you Sonic. I will never let you out again. Sonic has long teeth, a curvey tail, he has black and brown fur and is very somall

age 10   by sean Erasmus.

I Wish ....

I wish that I could fly over the world,
I wish there was no pollution,
I wish I wish I really wish that I was really rich.

Christopher Iliffe

What is a book?

A book is an Adventure into a different World
A book is a doorway for everyone to go through.
A book is fun like James and the giant peach.
A book is sad like black beauty.
When you are bored get a book
A book is exciting
A book is short
A book is long
A book is a journey through time.

by
Tom Ward. age 11.

My Extra Special day.

I wish I could play snooker with Ronnie O'Sullivan and beat him and pot all the balls in. And I will win the trophy.

Paul Smith.

The Lonsdale Monster.

At night when all the children have gone home
He walks the corridors all alone
His wide green eyes skimming every room
The whole school filled with dark, dark gloom
Searching for his prey
Yet he knows it will not be there until day
He peers through a hole in a wall
And watches the children in the hall.
With his long green legs and arms
And his smile with many charms
His long sleek finger grabbing anything which dare linger.
Until one night he heard a loud cry
Then a little boy caught his huge green eye
He walked up to the boy picked him up like a toy
He swallowed him whole
And all that was left was his bag and an old clothes tag.

by Elizabeth Shanahan age. 11

Anger

Anger is the colour of red
it burns like a fire.
Anger tastes like hot chillis
burning in your mouth.
Anger smells like onions
that make your mouth water.
Anger looks like blood that
makes you flush red.
Anger sounds like thunder
its like the roaring in your head.
Anger feels like rage.
So watch out when I am mad.

By James Scott
Age 10

when I grow up

when I grow up am going to be
a farmer. I will drive a tractor.
I will keep cows and sheep I will
have to milk the cows twice
a day. I think it will be great fun.
Andrew Thomas.

my school.

I like number work and I like the buildings
because they are a nice colour and I
like painting and I like reading in
the book corner and the school is very
colourful and the teachers are very nice
and I like like p.e. and I like history
and I like the playtime because it
is very big to play on and I like
dinner time because I like my dinner
and I like swimming very much.
by Kelly Buckley

My pet

I have a pet dog. Her name is Rosie. Her breed is a golden retriever. Rosie is two years old. On my birthday one of my friends left her jelly and ice cream on the side and Rosie nicked the jelly off the side and it was my friends favourite jelly

Lizzie Bailey
age 9
3/4S

My school

I like school because it is fun and you can play with the toys in the classroom. there is mobilo and the polydron and I like my classroom because I can do pe and I like dinner time. Thomas Fildes IJ

My Big Dog

My dog is a German Shepherd. You have never seen such a big dog his name is Jack. My dog is very funny. My friends are skared of him. On saturday a lady comes to see the ponies she goes down past Jack's run and scares her.

Kate Freshwater
age 9.

My School

I like the teachers in the school and my teachers is funny and all the teachers are kind, and we do number work I like it and I liked it when we went swimming with the school and play time is good and when it is diner time it is nice. by sarah Johnson

Why I like my classroom

I like my teacher and like doing my news and doing word bulding book and activities and painting

Thomas Mason IJ

When I grow up
When I grow up I want to be a space man so I can study the stars and the planets.
I can also take photos of things people have never seen before.
I will see comets and asteroids milkyways and cosmic space dust.
But best of all I can visit the moon.
by Matthew Feledziak.
age 8

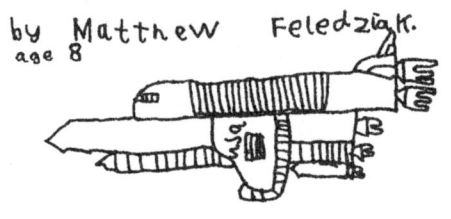

my school   by John Wilkes

I like my Sums and I like my dinner I like playtime and I like number work and I like going swimming and I like my friends because they play with me

when I grow up

When I grow up I am going to save some money to go to Florida again. I like shamau because he can splash 14 rows of seats. I saw two alligators in the wild and Five in the zoo.

Andrew Johnson
age 8

my class

I like school because I can do paintings and drawings and you can have so much fun and you can do funny stories and I like to play with the polydron.

by Vanessa James 15

I love playing outside and I like eating my break

CLaSSRF

me Sophie Danielle
caroline saton

I have One dog and One hamster and One rabbit. My chickens died five weeks ago. I'm very sad because they have always won first prize in the pet show every year. My dog's name is Tiffany We had two dogs in the past One ran away though. My hamsters name is Barry
We have had three hamsters in the past, my rabbit's name is Snowdrop because he is all black except for his nose

Nicola Cheadle   age 8 years old.

My bunny   My dog Tiffany

My hamster

The King

Tyrannosaurus
was the king,
He ruled the
dinosaurs,
He had sharp teeth
Thick strong legs
And mighty sharp
claws.
If he saw me
He would
have me for tea!!

Nicholas Feledziak

I Wish

Oh I wish the planet Terra (Earth) was a better place. No more war or hatred. If we had a world like this nobody would mind. But never can the world be like I want it to be.

Ryan Guest age 9

Our World

Peaceful world

My Extra Special Day

I want to go to the seaside. I want to go to the beach and I want to play in the sand. I want to make a sand castle and have a paddle in the sea.

Rebecca Hibbert

Seasons Poem

S pring has got.
P retty flowers.
R ed Roses.
I ce cold lollipops.
N aughty little children playing.
G reen, green grass.

T ime goes by
I ce cold again.
M en working in the cold.
E normous mountains covered in snow

By Catherine Shelley age 8

I wish......

I wish I was a cowboy.
I can have a hat on my
head and a belt on me. I can have
a horse to ride on.
I have two guns
and I can shoot the
guns.

Michael Constable.

I Wish

I Wish that people would not pollute the Sea. I hope that people do realise that when they throw things away that they go into the Sea and it affects animals and where they live. I just can't understand why we pollute the Sea and oceans.

Verity Bland 8

Laura Peak

I Like colouring pictures at school

class RF

I Wish

I Wish I was a person who could fly a fight Jet very fast through the sky and do stunts in theair. I Wish I could drive a Ferrarri. I Wish I could fly an aeroplane that carted people to different places. I Wish I could work on computers, and fix them. I Wish I could play a guitar and be in a choir.

Sebastian Hicks 8

I like playing in the shop at school

con her Jeffres classte

I wish I could go where I liked
I wish I could go to Africa
I wish I could go on holiday
I wish I could have own computer

William Ainsworth
8

Emily Fidgett class RH

I like playing skipping and hopscotch on the playground

I like playing pod on the computer

Myself

My name is Alex. Our family has a pet dog called Tess who is a Golden Labrador. I have a sister who is 8 and she has a pet hamster called hammy. I have dark hair and brown eyes. My sister irritates me and sometimes I feel mad. I would like to get a pet of my very own and I would like it to be a lizard. I enjoy football and other sports. I play football on Saturdays, and then on Sundays we have a match. In our class we are studying modern and Ancient Greece. We are finding the difference between Athens the capital of Greece, and Sparta in Ancient times. My favourite lessons at school are maths, Art and Craft. I am in the top maths Group and the top Ginn Group. My favourite food is Pizza. by Alex Leigh (age 10)

I like swimming Charlotte Smith best
I like drawing pictures at School

CLASS RH

Special times.

Here are some really special times. Firstly when my baby sister was born because I was a big sister. Secondly. When I went to Zoomarina to see the dolpins and sealions they both were brilant because of the stunts they did. The sealions did a concert and the dolphins flipped and went through rings. Thirdly I went to see TAKE THAT they were Amazing because I really like them and they did Summer Salt in the air. Foerthly When I got a bike and hamster for my Birthday.

by Danielle Witkowski
Age 10.

My pets

I have 3 pets 1 dog shes Black and white. Shes very lovely and she love playing for hours with me shes a great guard dog. She can tell when same one is not welcome. I have two birds they are girls. If they hear other blrds they start going teet teet and they do not shut up. one is bule and the other one is buley green.

Charlie
Baker

age 10

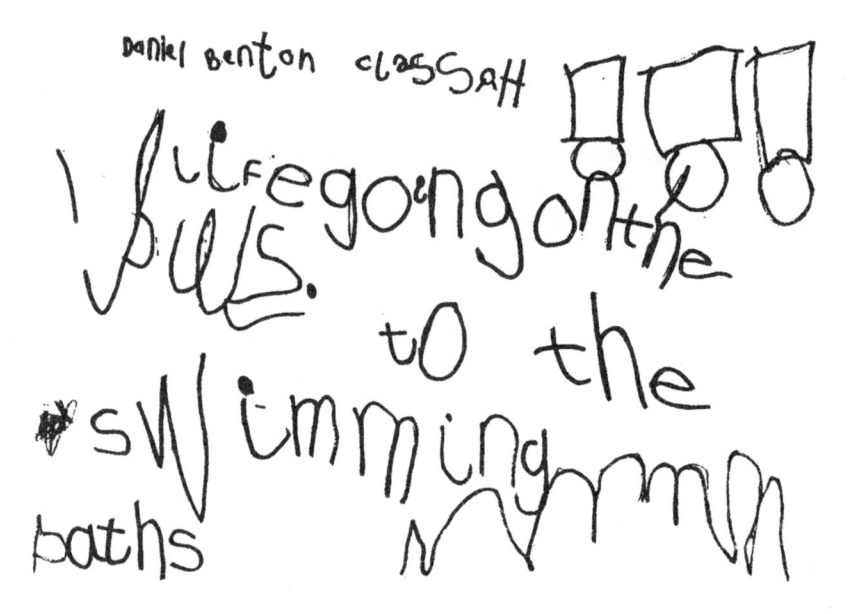

Daniel Benton class 5AH
I luv life going on the buss. to the swimming baths

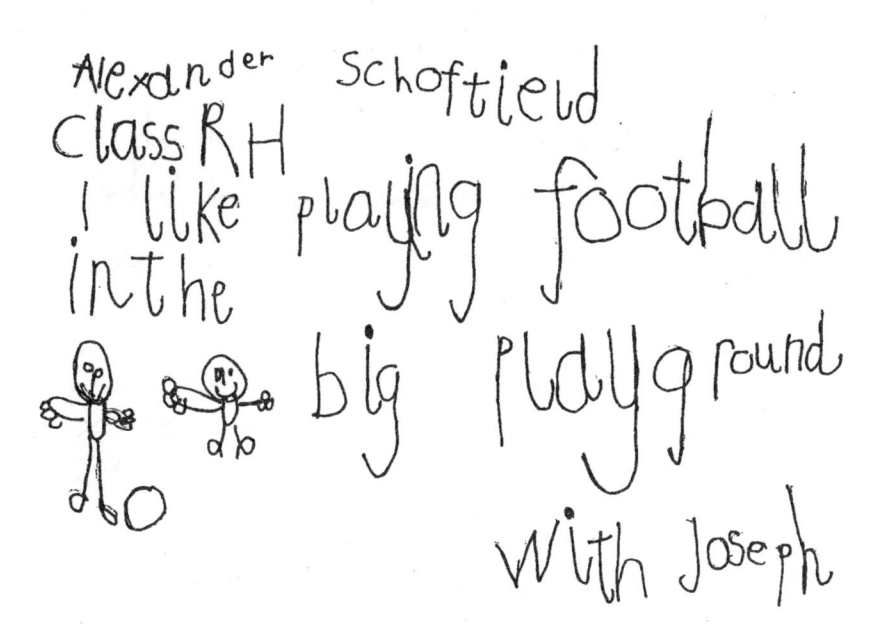

Alexander Schoftield
Class RH
I like playing football in the big playground with Joseph

Crimson berries on the hedges,
Rong leaves starting to drop off the trees
Bouds of Emerald leaves on the road
Oh yes, lets go out and play
Under the leaves and play,
Run and what crunch it makes,
Sigh of happiness its Autumn.

by Ian Maitland
age 9.

Red

Red is my best colour. It is not at the End of my colour list. It is good. I like Doing things with red paint. — James Willshaw

SPACE

Stars shooting,
Planets turning and flashing,
Asteroids flying by,
Comets whizzing past planets,
Earth below,

Space men on the moon,
Hot sun cold moon,
In a spaceship earth is so faraway,
Planets flash,
Stars twinkle in space,

By Steven Edwards.
Age nine.

SPACE SON MOON EARTH

PLUTO NEPTUNE URANUS

VENUS MERCURY MARS SATURN JUPITER

When I grow up I am going to be a teacher to teach children how to do their numbers. Claire Parry

Victoria
Matthew Sclass srF

I like
playing
at
school
oo
outside

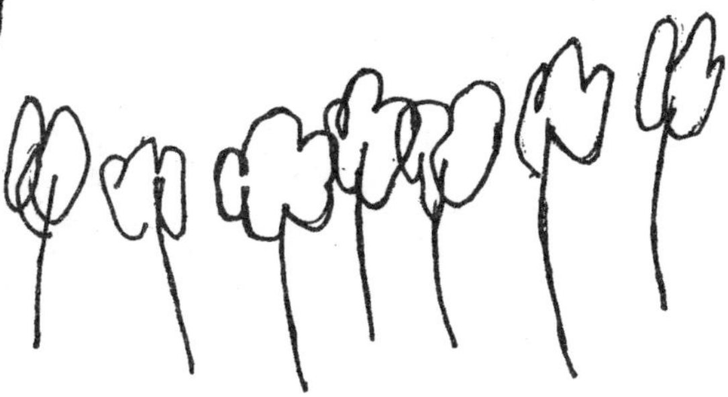

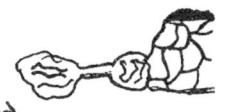

vegtabel garden

I wish I could go where I liked.
I wish I could go to Wales.
I wish it was the summer holidays.
I wish I could have my own computer.
I wish I could have my own pets.
I wish I could have my own bedroom.
       Leian Constable. 9.

CLASS RF

Benjamin James
I like playing with the mobilo at school

I wish....
I wish there was no fighting and no-one killing each other. If nobody killed each other the world would be a better place.

Jane Shanahan. 8.

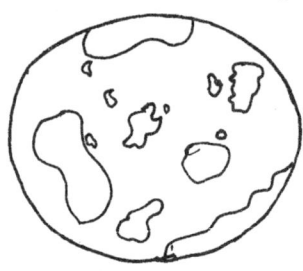

I like playing with the lego at school

class RF

Thomas Hibbert

I Love.

I love animals very, very much, my favourite animals in the whole wide world are Dogs and Puppies. But I still like other animals. At the moment I have a Puppy but he'll be one year old soon. His name is Barney and I love him very much.

Katie Philcox. 9.

Animal Friend

My Animal friend was an albino rabbit with red eyes. We called him red eyes he had a cold and died. There was a hole in the roof of his hutch we put a board on it but the rain still got in. He was only one year old. He would lick the cage when he saw me. When I stroked him he ran in and out of the hutch. He was always jumping too high and nearly banging his head. I miss him a lot We had 29 rabbits then.

Sarah Anne Evans
Age 10

I want to be a tennis player because I like tennis. I want to go in the Finals For England

Joel McGowan

Special Times

A special time for me was when I went to Lindos in Greece because my dad and I wanted to go and see the Acropolis up in the mountains. We wanted to go and see it because we had heard alot about it and that it was a beautiful sight. Both of us wanted to see where the Ancient Greek Gods used to sit. When we were walking up some steps next to us was a ship which had been carved into a wall. When we got to the top of the Acropolis we could see down into the sea. It was a long way down. On the top there were millions of rocks and pebbles as though a wall had caved in. On the way down we travelled on donkeys which was fun.

By
Steven Darlington
age 10

I Wish.

I wish to go to Africa because I can get a sun tan and there are beaches and there are very good people there are hotels there too

by Terry Warrelow
age 10

ccleste plant
classrH
ilike swimming

Animal friends

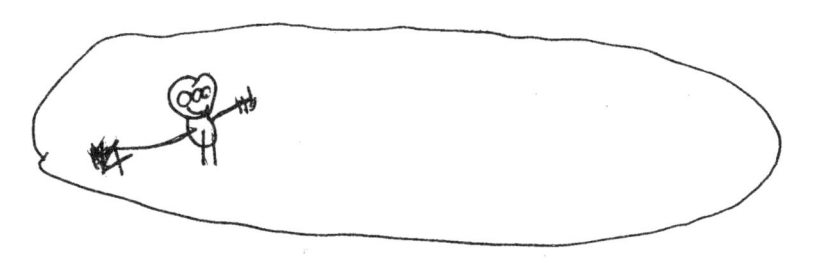

I have two cats their names are Dylan and Alfie. They are both ginger tom cats. Dylan has more white fur than Alfie but Alfie is more fussy about being stroked. They both bite sometimes. Dylan likes water, he puts his paws on the edge of the bath when I'm in it. Alfie sometimes sleeps on the cushion on the corner of the settee. Dylan and Alfie sometimes sleep on the spare bed sometimes both at the bottom, sometimes both at the top, sometimes one at each end. They run off when someone sits on my bean bag because of the noise that the beads in it make. They are both brothers and are 3 years old.

by
Alison Davies
age 10.

Dylan   Alfie

Blue is?

Blue is a water fall,
Like tap water,
Under sun light,
Even the sky is blue.

David Trigg

My Hobby.

Football is my hobby,
Of all the sports there are,
Only one satisfies me, football,
Tottenham, Man utd, Villa and wolves,
Brilliant teams
And rubbish ones too,
Look at Dwight Yorke what a player
Look at football what a game.

by Robbie Lennox
age 9 3/45

Yellow

A sun set sky
A dancing daffodil
A swaying tulip
Some melted butter
Some cheese
A peeled banana
Some blossom
Some leaves

Emily Goodwin

My Pirate

My pirate has black curly hair. My pirate has got one big ear and a small ear. My pirate has black eye brows. He has big fat blue eyes. He has a big spiky nose. My pirate has one tooth. He has hair on his face and its black beard. He is fat and short. Hes got a dagger and a sword and, hes got two arms and one wooden leg.

by Christian Shepherd

age 8

By Westley Constable age 11

The Ant and the Puddle

An ant was running very quickly down the wide pavement. Then suddenly someone said "Get off." The ant looked down and saw an angry rippling puddle. The ant said he was very sorry and leapt out quickly. He went everyday to the puddle and talked to him, until one day it was extremely hot and the sun had evaporated the puddle. When the ant came along that afternoon you could imagine his face. He was very upset and miserable. For three whole days the ant sat there without food or water until that night he died. And the first drops of rain fell on him. It was too late.

Happiness

Happiness is the colour of red; like a big smile all happy and warming.
Happiness tastes of delicious cream buns with chocolate swirls and sugar strands.
Happiness smells like a beautiful red rose with bees buzzing in and out.
Happiness looks like a cheerful face laughing and joking with friends.
Happiness sounds like lots of children having fun running around and playing games.
Happiness feels like a small puppy all fluffy and soft with a cold wet nose.
So that's why....
Happiness makes me feel better when I'm sad or angry.

Elizabeth Austin   age 11

Red

Red is the apple,
Red is a flowers,
Red is the blossom,
Red is stop,
Red is a colour,
Red is a rose.

Anna Busby.

When I grow up I would like to work at a hospital and I would like to be a nurse

Katie Davies

Red

Red is a rose,
Red is a strawberry,
Red is a poppy,
Red is a berry,
Red is a apple.

Carly Tambos

Planets.

Planets floating in the sky,
Lively comets zooming,
Asteroids in a belt,
Neptune, a lovely blue colour,
Earth, with sea and land,
Tiny yellow dwarfs and huge red giants,
Somtimes I wonder about these things.

by Helena Brooks aged 9

When I grow up I would like to be a farmer because I like animals.
          Kim Robinson.

My pirate

My pirate's got hair thats all sticking out and he's got black hair. He hasn't got very big ears. He's got big bushy eyebrows and they're black. He's got big brown eyes and he's got two eyes. A long pointy blue nose. He's got four black teeth. He's got a black hairy face. He's small and plump. He's got a short dirty T-shirt he's wearing dirty jean's and he's got two arms and two legs and a long sharp sword.
by Gemma Frank S.   age 8.

Green

A summer tree,
A field full of grass,
A stem of a flower,
A grape,
A prickly bush,
An apple,
A tree with apple blossom
          Charlotte Secker

My Colour Poem

Blue is the sea,
Blue are the waves,
Blue is the sky,
Blue is rain,
Blue is the blue bell,
Blue is the forget-me-not

Daniel Topley.

forget-me-not

sea

← Blue Bells

Planets

P is for Planets so dull and so bright,
L is for lively comets, so dark and so light,
A is for astronaut so white and so excited,
N is for nothing so silent and still,
E is for Energy that makes you float,
T is for thousands of shooting stars,
S is for space so quiet and still

By Emily Rigg aged eight

Happiness

Happiness is the colour of red. the colour of cherries on a cake.
It tastes of a sweet rosy apple sitting in a tree.
It smells of sweet flowers, blooming in a garden bright and beautiful.
Happiness looks like a big smily face with twinkling eyes.
Happiness sounds like people having a laugh with dimples in their cheaks as they smile.
Happiness is a clown at a circus making you laugh.
Happiness is the best gift of all.

Gemma Newman
age 10.

Dean Key
age 11

The Dreaded Birthday Kiss

I'll never forget that day the bell rang and seemed to almost shatter the school windows. It was dinner time! There I was trambling in my shoes in the dinner line. Phew! I've made it past Mrs Rossant, but will I make it past the others? We'll find out soon enough It's a very challenging sport this. I've past one, no two, I've got my dinner. Touch down! I'm working as fast as I can. All finished I dive for the door. Oh! no! Mrs cooper comes in with a big sloppy kiss like a dog drooling. Shes got me. Watch out kids. Mrs cooper could be coming to your school, when its your birthday!

Fred The Talking dog

Katie Batten age 11

My lazy big dog Fred, is alway sleeping in my bed
He's always getting in the way and never, never will
obey. Then I'd really had enough so I began to get tough
BUT
The very next day I was taking him for a walk
When suddenly he began to talk.
"SIT!" I said. "NO!" replied Fred.
So I hit him with a key
And he ran up a very tall tree.
"Come Back!" I shouted.
It was no good I could climb up if I could
Then slowly down he came when I quietly called his name,
I took him home but he wasn't fed and he had to
go straight to bed.
And ever since the dreadful day.
He always did obey.

LATE by THOMAS HARDY AGE 11

I burst out of the still sleeping house, flying all the way to school, shouting "I'm LATE! I'm LATE!" I got to school breathless and I heard singing coming from the hall. It was the school assembly. Then I slowly walked upto the hall door thinking the teacher was going to put me in detention. A burst of fear was pulling me back as I walked into the hall. She was there! She came towards me and was kind of smiling for some reason. When she got to me she said, "Hello Thomas a bit late aren't you?" As soon as she said that I felt a smile coming up on my face. I was not going to be in detention after all so I went to sit down in a place by my friends, feeling happy.

Muffin

I have a smooth-haired rabbit
Her name is Muffin
She is grey and white
And eats carrots and greens
She is a Harlequin rabbit
I got her when she was 12 weeks old
It was a late birthday present
My sister made a wooden hutch
With doors both side and front
For my Harlequin rabbit
When its lovely and warm
She goes to the willow tree
She will eat the green leaves of it
The washes her face with her paws
My lovely Harlequin rabbit.

Rebecca Mart   6H

Curiosity

Curiosity is the colour of orange,
Like the golden sun in the evening shining behind the wall of trees.
It tastes like an egg when its cracking open on your plate and you find a chick inside.
It smells like chocolate in your birthday present, rich and sweet, you can't wait to open it.
It looks like the worlds biggest secret, have you heard it? Of course not its a secret.
It sounds like the noises under the floor, the thumping, the bumping keeping you awake.
It feels like the lumps hiding under wrapping paper.
You shake it, you finger it, until at last
Curiosity gets the better of you and you rip it open

Amy Palmer   age 10

Wild mad wilderbeest
Indanger of becoming extinct
Lots of mad monkeys
Dangerous wild dogs
Abandoned Jungles
Nasty wild lions
Intelligent little beasts
Miniature flying beetles
Angry prowling tigers
Long tall strong giraffes
Scaly slithery snakes

Overgrown forests, African plains,
Hot dry deserts, muddy swamps

These can be home to
Wild Animals

BY James Ainsworth aged 11

My Favourite Player

He is brilliant because he is the best defender in the world and he plays for the best team in the world, Stoke City. Ian Cranson is 31 years old and he is brilliant at football. I wish I was as good at football as he is, but I'm not. I think he is brilliant because no player can get past him without him taking the ball off them and when he's got the ball he passes it up the field with his left foot and brilliant aim. I think he should get picked for the England squad. I'd pick him if I could. If Stoke did not have him they would get relegated. He is brilliant.

Daniel Aston.

Age 11.

My School

The good thing about coming into school is that it is the same old classroom the teachers are nice too.

By Richard Rimington 1J

Miss Jones

Racing cars.

Red, Green its go! Damon Hill up to the first corner. Murray Walker goes bonkers in the commentary box as Jonathan Palmer talks us through the start. Loads of crashes and smashes and burning rubber. In for tyres and fuel goes Hill as Frank Williams watches on. Hill in the Williams Renault car storms out of the pit lane. He's past the Ferrari of Eddie Irvine into 6th. Now he's passing Michael Schumacher. A great manoeuver by Hill. Jean Alesi is slowing down with a blown engine. Thats 4th for Hill and now he's closing on Rubens Barrichello. While Barrichello is in the pits Hill goes ahead, Berger is the next target. Berger is out he's spun out. Jacques Villeneuve is 1st as Hill is hot on his tail. Its the last lap who is going to win? Hill passes Jacques Villeneuve. What a win!

By Matthew Knopp. Age 9.

my teacher.

I like my teacher. she makes me laugh. and she is funny.

By Lewis Holdcroft 1J

Miss Jones

Formula One.

Ferrari, Williams, Benetton and Ford.
Over the race track the commentators are going wild.
Ruebens Barchelli and Jean Alesi.
Micheal Schumacher and Damon Hill.
Unbelievable noises coming from the cars.
Lives nearly come to an end when the cars spin.
Awesome speeds of 300mph.

Only one person wins the race its Damon Hill.
Nobody stays dry on the podium with champagne.
Everybody gets soaked.

By Jack Boulton.
age 9

My school

I like my teacher and I play
I like painting and I like
polydron and I like playing
in the home corner.

by Jack Lockett
Miss Jones

When I grow up

When I grow up I want to be a scientist so I can study things and mess around with chemicals and try not to blow myself up. I would be like the mad scientist who wears a white coat and has crazy ideas.

Daniel Morris
age 8

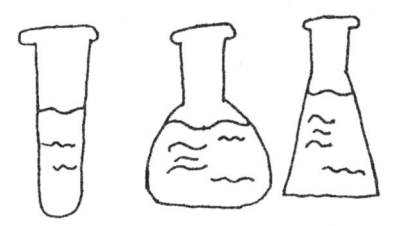

My Pets

I had been begging my mum for ages to have my own rabbit and my mum finally gave up and brought me a rabbit. After abit my rabbit got lonley so we brought my sister a rabbit. My rabbit didn't like my sisters and bit it. We put them in seperate cages. My dad has always wanted a dog. We have got a dog now he is brown and white. When we first got him he was nervous. He is alot better now. Every time I see him after school he jumps up on me. I love my pets.

by Claire Edwards
age 8

When I grow up

When I grow up I want to be a potter. Putting the clay on the potters wheel and making lots of things. Like big vases and little pots for flowers then I would carve little pictures on them. Then I would paint them with special paint so it won't come off. On childrens birthdays I will put the persons name on the pot and fill it with sweets. On grown ups birthdays I will fill the pot with things.

by William Leigh

My School

I like my school because the work is easy and I like my school because I can do drawings and I like to go on the bus to school.

By Alex Lennox 1st

My cat

I have got a cat. We have not chosen a name yet. It is ten weeks old. When it goes upstairs it looks very funny. When it goes up it hops like a rabbit when it comes down it is like a racing car.

LIAM Edgar

my class

I like my class because I like doing number work and because I like my teacher and p.e; and I like my play times because I like playing with Becky and Kelly and Hannah Silcox and I like writing and I like reading and I like history and I like my dinner times.

By Sarah Kempster.

Jumping Jack Flash

Jumping Jack Flash is a dog but not just any dog. He can do things other dogs cannot do He can walk on his back legs for 10 minutes and can stay in the air for 15 seconds. Jumping Jack Flash can run as fast a Linford christie, cam chatch a ball with his legs, play football like Ryan Griggs. That's why I called him Jumping Jack Flash.

by Robert Snow
Age 10

I wish..

I wish that I could have a horse so I can ride to school.

Susan Shepherd.

Oscar Oscar you bright sun
You are like fire glowing in the night
You roll on the ground like Spinning Wheel
You are round like bouncy balls
You are as round as a football
You roll-spinning round and round and round.

Rebecca Archer.

I wish

I wish that I could take over all the F.1 racing teams and I would buy all the best mechanics.

Freddie Lawton

My holiday

I went on holiday once with my mum and my dad and my sister and also, some of my mum and dads' friends with their son Sam. We went to Butlins in wales. We had separate rooms but every morning we met in the canteen. Then we would go out for the day. At a place one night we were all having a drink and the fire alarm went off. My uncle Burt was in the toilets with Sam when it happened and that scared Mandy. My mum was in the next room ordering pizza and that worried me. But in the end it was only some children messing about, so there was no problem. When my mum had the pizza we went back to our room and ate it.

Laura Davies age 9.

Once my hamster looked as if it was dead but it was still breathing. It had its eyes closed. I gave it some food and left it for a few minutes. I went and got some more food and when I went in it was lively. My hamster was alright, I was so pleased.

Bobbie-Jo Davies 8

I wish....
I wish I could play for Aston Villa because I would like to meet Dwight York. I would like to play and score for Villa.

Joshua Dawson.

I Wish.......
I wish I could be a princess because instead of me getting a drink the servants would get one for me.

Lara Beardmore.

I wish .....

I wish that at break time people would not throw litters because it makes our school untidy

Wish

I wish I could go up into space in a rocket and step on the moon. And see the sun and all the stars. And see the flag on the moon and float off into space and see Mars and all the other planets

Christopher Mart
age 9

sarah prinolol
I Like the
wind at school
CLASS RF

I wish

I wish the world was a better place, no pollution, litter or rubbish I wish people wouldn't be so careless about where they put their litter. If it is put into the sea it polutes the sea and the animals that live in it. If it is dropped in the country side it makes the country side look messy and ugly.

Joe Hyatt .9.

Robert Brooks Class RH
I like playing

Myself

I have hazel eyes and I have ginger hair. I am 9 years old and I like making things with my dad like cars, boats and motorbikes. I have a kind personality and I like going to Stapley Water Gardens. I also like cooking different kind of food. When I grow up I am going to be a wildlife photographer.

by
David Pearce aged 9 years

William Perks

I would like to be a policeman and ride a motor bike and I will catch a burglar

I Wish ???

I wish to go to a wonderful place called Disneyland in florida were your dreams come true and to see the amazing characters and the amazing films. I would like to play a game of golf with Goofy, Micky, Mini and Donald duck. There brillant shops and the brillant rides. I would like to see the midnight parads and see the lovely clothes the characters wear.

by - Rachel Davies
age 10

Emma-Jane Busby class RH

I like doing my work. I enjoy Maths best of all

Animal Friend

I have a very special pet. She has brown eyes and she is black all over. She has four white paws and a bit of white on her neck. She has a long tail and her hair is about an inch long. She has a black nose. Her name is Bea she is my dog.

by
Stephen Lockley Age 9

Animal Friends

My pets are, 2 cats, a snake, 2 skinks and a chinchilla. Our cats were our first pets and they're names are salt and pepper. They are twins and are 3 years old. Our snake has been lost because there were a lot of holes in his cage. Our skinks are a type of lizard, a bit like eels on legs. They are DISGUSTING. They're quite new to James my step brother, and he loves unusual pets. Next he wants an Iguana. The chinchilla is soft grey and has got a tail like a propeller and is very sweet.

by Kate Mohin
Age 10

LUCY
KURT
COBAIN
SALT PEPPER
CHARLIE

I want to be a footballer and scare lots of goals to win the game

philip oyatt.

Benjamin middleton
class RH

I like playing outside on the grass and I like going swimming

Breezy Day,
Every day it gets chillier,
really damp,
really foggy,
Its Windy,
Every day gets shorter,
So misty.

Jodie Ford
age 9

Alexandra Alcock
Class RH

I Like playing hospitals

Autumn

Laura Goodban
aged 9.

Crispy crunchy autumn leaves,
Blowing gently in the breeze,
Whirling twirling round and round,
Then they fall on to the ground,
It's misty dull and rather damp,
And not a very nice place to camp.

Timothy Dudley
class JRH
I like playing football at school

when I grow up I would like to be a footballer because I would play in the playground and I would like to be in aston villas team

owen Archer

Woke playing a t school
thther aby

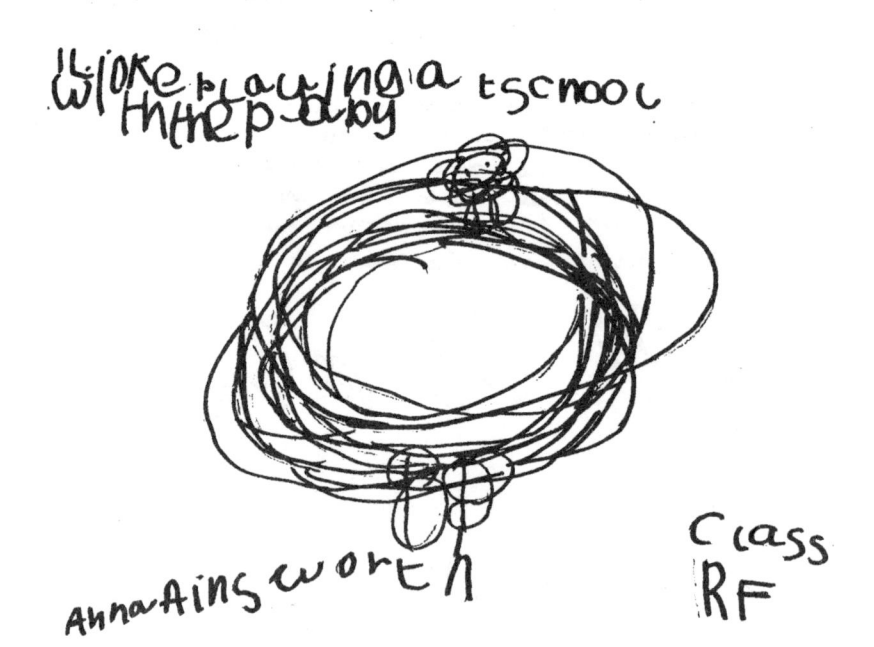

Anna Ainsworth

Class RF

I wish

I wish I could bungee jump off a waterfall.
The waterfall would be 100 foot high
and 20 foot wide.
I wish I could ride on a pony
The pony would be dappled-gray
and the pony and I would ride across fields.
   Rosalund
   Wiggins

ClassR F

I Like making models with the mobilo at school

James Carruthers

We went to the market and we got a Tazo folder and we got a ball. We went down to the park and we saw my friend, his name is Matthew. We went to play. He is my best friend. We played on the rope and we went on the slides. We went to get some sweets, they were 10p each. Matthew got me one with his money. We had a lollipop and then we got the dog he jumped up at us. It was a nice day

Rory Key 7

Jack Lawton
I like playing with
the duplo
at school   Jack

classre

I wish

I wish I had a pony that could fly through the clouds. I would like to feel the wind on my face and look down on fields and houses.
Victoria Ann Talbot 8

When I grow up I want to be a nurse because I want to make people better and help them when they are in trouble and I can make friends with them Gemma Humphries

A Special Time

It was the usual boring Tuesday morning until we got into the car and drove off to Cadburys World. At Cadburys World we got a questionnaire and a creme egg. Inside Cadburys World we filled in the questionnaire. Half way through the tour we got a Time Out and then saw how the chocolate was made (it looked rather sickly) and then we got a Dairy Milk bar. After we went into the Fantasy Factory and looked at things. I am 49 fudge bars tall and they make 300 million Creme Eggs a year and two hundred 200 gram Dairy Milk bars a minute (thats alot). At about 3 o'clock we went in the play area then into the museum. That was my brilliant day at Cadburys World.

by
Paul Swaries
age 10

When I grow up

When I grow up I don't really know what I want to do, job wise, but I would like to travel round the world or to as many different countries as possible. I might get a job to earn some money then go to one country, come back to England, get another job to earn some more money, go to a different country etc. I also play the cornet so I would like to become famous on it and have a stretch limo to get around in, but I suppose we will have to wait and see.

by Michael Ball
Age 10

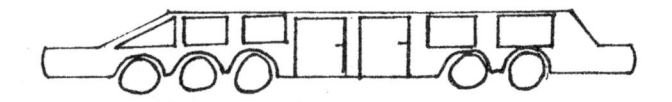

Myself

Hello my name is Gemma Hilton I live at Brook House Castle Street Eccleshall. I am jolly, kind, good, generous and I lend things to people. Sometimes I'm good tempered sometimes I'm bad tempered. I'm a great daydreamer, I dream at night, and in the day. My best friends are Miranda, Alison, Sarah, Kelly, and Leanne. My eyes are blue and I have brown hair, and I have to wear glasses. When its spring time I get a cold, It comes every year and I have hayfever and a cough.

by Gemma Hilton. Age 10

My Pet

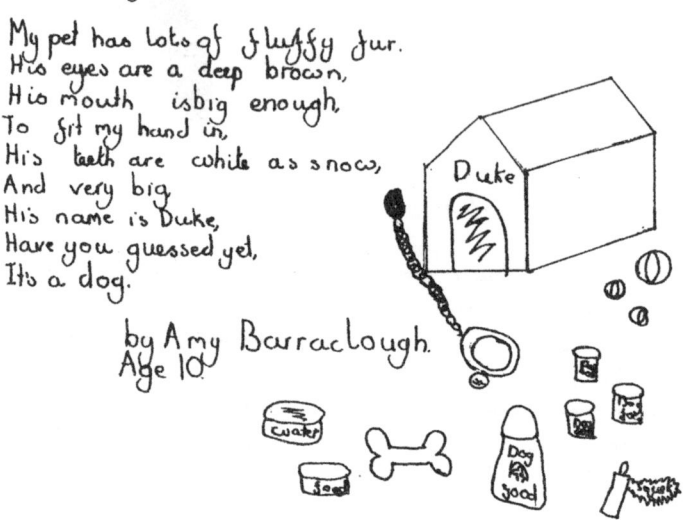

My pet has lots of fluffy fur.
His eyes are a deep brown,
His mouth is big enough,
To fit my hand in,
His teeth are white as snow,
And very big,
His name is Duke,
Have you guessed yet,
It's a dog.

by Amy Barraclough.
Age 10

when I Grow up I am going to be a farmer and I am going to have a dog

Thomas Constable

My Pirate

My pirate has bobbed curly hair with small and one ear big. He also long and rather hairy eyebrows. He's got big round bulging eyes one blue one brown. My pirate also has got a star shape nose. He's got yellow teeth but he's only got ten teeth. My pirate has got smelly pongy breath. He's got a big curly black beard. He's round, podgy and short. My pirate wears big black trousers. A red shirt with silver buttons popping off. My pirate also has a dagger He wears a head scarf and an earing. He's got an arm in the middle of his chest and he's got one wooden leg and one proper leg.

Sarah Holland aged 8

Green

the green grass is blowing in the wind,
The green apples on a tree,
The green leaves dancing on the branches.

James Foxley

MATCH

Footballers

McClair has been fouled and it's a penalty.

A penalty to Manchester United and Cantona has scored.

The match has kicked off again.

Craig Short has equalised for Everton.

He's scored – Andy Cole has scored!

by Thomas Hammond age 8.

Red

Red is an apple,
Red is fire,
Red is a bus,
Red is a strawberry,
Red is an Autumn leaf
Red is a bird

Lauren Brook Archer

a strawberry   a apple   a fire

Green

Green are the buds on the trees,
Green is the grass,
Green is the outside of a water melon,
Green is an apple,
Green are leaves in the spring,
Green is a holly leaf.

Louise Alice Mathews

Autumn

Colours are yellows
and orang and red
Leaves went rustle
on the wind who
rustle up into the any
and it rustle in the
wind and some
tthes the wind stops.

by Dean Littlehales
Aar 8

Red

poppies growing,
A juicy apple,
Cooking tomato,
Burning sun tan.

Thomas Alcock

The Haunted House

One day I went to see the Haunted House in the end of the forest with my frind called Tom. Me and Tom went there all the time. When we got there we went in because the door was open. We went up stairs and the floorbards creaked and Tom jumped because they creaked again and then we went up stairs. We got to the top of the stairs and we checked the bedroom out again and then we saw the door shut on it's own. So we ran down stairs and went outsie and ran home. When we got home we heard a bang from the Haunted House.

by Matthew Newman
age 8

Red

Red is a rose,
Red is some blood,
Red is an apple,
Red is a strawberry,
Red is some flowers,
Red is a rosy cheek,
Red is a tan.

Lisa Erasmus

Autumn

Leaves go purple
Emeralds are bright green.
Apples falling off the trees
Very many leaves on the floor
Exciting when the leaves go around
Some leaves are changing colour

by
michael Rogers
age 8

My Colour poem
Black as night,
Black as a forest,
Black as leather,
Black as a chalk board,
Black as a tv.

Jack Simpson

L ight out side
E merald green grass
A utumn is fun
V icars christening babies
E very bird appears
S un vanishes, wind comes
by Teri 7

when I grow up I would like to be
a zookeeper because I like animals. I would
like to be the trainer and babysitter all of
the animals.

louise wood

My pirate

My pirate has got smelly black hair and one ear. He's got long black eyelashes and one big red eye. And he's got a snotty nose and five teeth and they're yellow and brown. He has a black hairy face and he's short and fat. He's got a dagger and he's dressed in rags he has got a wooden leg and he's lost two fingers.

By Scott Walker
Age 9

yellow
yellow banana,
yellow lemon,
yellow sun,
yellow daffodil

Corrina Gumbley

Yellow

Yellow is the sun,
Yellow is the daffodil,
Yellow is melted butter,
Yellow is the cheese,
Yellow is the banana,
Yellow is the lemon,
Yellow is the leaf,
Yellow are the chicks,

Carolyn Rippon

Thomas Simpson
age: 9

The wicked witch

Once upon a time there lived a terrible witch called Winney. Winney made the evilest poisons in the land. Her latest poison was one that turns you into an elf. Winney sells her poisons at the village market. She say's they keep you alive forever. The witch makes alot of money out of them. But Winney wasn't going to sell her new poison. One night Winney was looking for some more spider legs in a back street. Sudenly two boys jumped out from behind some dustbins and tried to pinch Winney new poison. Just before they could grab it Winney threw the poison all over the two boys and they started to transform into elfs

Daniel Mart
age. 9

The Wicked Witch

Once upon a time there lived a Wicked Witch. She made magic spells that can change people into different sorts of animals. She had a Wonkey nose And an old hat. The Witch had a big bag full of spell books and pouchs and a Wond. The Wicked Witch tested the spells on animals. And strange things happened to the animals

My pirate

my pirate is a mean old pirate. He has long curly black hair and long crusty brows one big harry brown nose. two big slimy dirty red teeth. A big face with red and green spots. He is very snappy and his shert is all slimey and his trousers have holes in he has one wooden leg and a dagger

alex hodson

Crazy Cat   by Sean Nyatt age 11

Normal cats would try to get into a mouse cage, but no, not my cat he just sits there staring at it. He's probably trying to death. (I hope it works) Most cats sleep in cat baskets, but no, no, my cat has to be abnormal, you know where sleeps? He sleeps among our newly washed duvets!

My cat has his own sort of sign language. His way of saying "feed me", is sitting dangerously on bannister and and staring wide eyed at you. And you know, I could have him there for half an hour and when I come back he'll still be there. If my cat wants stroking he sticks his sleek head through the narrow gap in the bannister and purrs loudly. When I was little I stuck my head in, but I almost got it stuck, and my head hurt for about a week afterwards. So I don't try to copy my cat.

Happiness

Happiness is red, yellow and other bright colours.
It is like a big red apple.
Happiness tastes like sugary sweets
and mouth watering strawberries.
Happiness smells like fresh honey
and newly baked cakes.
Happiness looks like a gigantic GALAXY chocolate bar
with my name on it!
Happiness sounds like lots of people laughing
and birds cheeping.
Happiness makes me feel like someone has just bought me
A horse, A Palimino of course.

```
    HAPPINESS.         .HAPPINESS.
       H                   S
     A                       S
     P                     E
       P                 N
         I           I
```

By Catherine
Dove
age 11.

Bonfire Night

Did you hear a banger shoot
up into the sky?
Did you see a catherine wheel
With all the gold on?
Did you see the fire burn up
the sky?
Did you hold a sparkler
With all the yellow stars?.

Daniel Migdal

What is a book

A book is fun, you enjoy.
A book is sad, you cry.
A book is adventerous, you smile.
A book is short, you sigh
A book is long, read on
A book is going places, hurry
A book is joyful, praise.
A book is funny, laugh.
A book is happy, cheer.
A book is here.
A book is there.
A book is everwere.

BY Christopher Joseph AGED 11

I wish......

I wish that I was a teacher because every day after school I play schools. At Christmas Santa brought me a blackboard. I get one of my big dolls and my brother. I like to teach people.

Megan Essery.

When I grow up.

When I grow up I would like to be a writer and write about animals like Beatrix Potter did I think they are quite good. My favourite animal is Jemima puddle Duck. If I can not be a writer I would like to be a singer because I like singing and I like music.

Kirsty Griffin
age 3/45

I like school because I like playing with my friends and I like playing with Lego and I like reeading books
Neil Forrester

My hobbies

My hobbies are horse riding, gymnastics and collecting Mr Men books and Little Miss books. I collect Mr Men and Little Miss books because I think that some of them are funny. I play the recorder and I'm going to play the cornet. I also like to play foot ball with my brother and my dad. I'm also going to play tennis at Eccleshall tennis club.

by Amy Swaries
age 8

Why I Like School

I like school because of the stories we have in assembly and also because of our beautiful class room and because of my lovely kind teacher and I love to have a few little play times as well and I also love to play with some of the activities and I love to do some colouring and reading and to lots of writing and also to do some number work, and history and I really love to do P.E, and swimming and I like the dinner ladies and my friends and everything.

MISS JONES.   by Charlotte Farnworth 1J

My Hobbies

My hobbies are swimming and horse riding I like swimming because it exercises my arms and legs. I go swimming at Riverside and I go horseriding on Holiday I like horse riding Because I like it when it shakes it's head and when it galiaps.

by Samantha Byatt
Age 9

The Pet

The pet is a dog I Love her a lot
her name is Honey she is golden.
every day Honey is naughty.

Pets are good to play with.
every morning I play with her
Tea time is Honeys best part of the day.

Rachel Johnson

7 and a big bit

3\4S

My friends.
I like my friends because they play with me
and I also like my friends because they
play silly games with me and some times
they come to my house and some times
I go to their house and they sit
be side me and also I like school
because I like my teacher and I also
like my school because we do interesting
things and I like doing number work and
I like doing p.e. By Becky Spennewyn. J.

When I grow up

When I grow up I would like to be a vet and help animals. I would like to help animals because I care for them. I would have to go to college and work hard.

By Sarah-Jane Duchney.

why I like my scool.

I like my scool because I've got lots of friends and work and I love my teacher because she gives me good work

by Hannah Bukon

When I grow up

When I grow up I would like to be a professionl football player for Aston Villa. My favourite player is Savo milosovic, my second favourite player is Dwight yorke.

By Richie Butler
age 8

Can you Guess?

Going to the librarey is were I'll be
Reading the top selfs is were I'll be
over the other ones is were I'll be
we are all over the world is were I'll be
I am some times long I am some times short
Nothing can be frightning or funny like me
Getting better getting worse is your choice

Under the cover of history is were I'll be
perhaps you know what I am?

by Lewis Jones

My classroom

I like my teachers and I like doing work and I like number work and I like going home on the bus and I like going to saool.

By Christabel Scott. U

my work

Miss Jones

my number work

the bus

I like school because Laura is sometimes here and Vanessa sometimes is here and I like the teacher. By Amy Collins

my pet
I have got a hamster She clumbs up the side of the cage. She is Syrian. Her name is Zan-cu-ie. Zancuie rolls around in her ball when I am cleaning her out. She bashes into things and the ball comes open.

Tim Jackson
Age 9

I Wish......
I Wish the World was made of chocolate and I could live in a chocolate house. Then I could make a chocolate cake and eat chocolate all the time.

Aimee Nicholls.

IF I were a dog.

IF I was a dog I would run and jump and hop as fast as I could. I would hate to be alon on my own. IF I saw my owner I would run jump and hop like a kangeroo to him and when I got to him I would wiggle my brown and white tail at him. Then I would hope he would give me a treat I would shake my long flo ppy ears when he stroked me. I would have my favourite chunky meat then after he would take me for a wkark all over the fields. Then I would go in and while he was watching TV I would be in my basket, getting tired then fall asleep. What a happy dog I would be.

James shaw

age 10

That Nasty Cat

There is a cat called Patch.
Who is so very nasty.
His sleek black and white fur sparkles in the sun.
He scratches me as I walk by.
And at night when I'm fast asleep.
He pounces on me and bites me.
He chases the dog and hunts for mice.
He's a mean old cat, hes not very nice.

Becky Clark
aged 11

I wish......
I wish I could watch wembley play.

I wish I could go on holiday and live there.

I wish I could be a fire lady.

Amie Sindefield.

NEWCASTLE F.C
I wish

I wish I wish I wish

I wish that I could play for Newcastle football club when I grow up, is I could not I would like to be an athlete because I really like running and it keeps me fit.

Martin Hall 9

My Extra-Special Day

I would like to go and play for Manchester United. It will be at a football stadium for children. And my friends can play too.

Oliver Snape.

My pets

My pets are special to me. I have two cats, two fish and a rabbit. I am going to talk about my cats. I have got a cat called AL, my brother's cat is called Jaz. Jaz is like a dog, She follows My mum, my brother and me everywhere. AL is a bit silly. He goes outside for one minute and then he wants to come back in. Jaz sleeps on my bed and AL sleeps on my brother's bed. Jaz is the one who comes up to school. Jaz got hit by a car two weeks after we got her.

by Frances McGowan
age 8.

My pond

> In my pond there are seven goldfish called Bubble, Shark, Julies Goldie, Mark, Jam, Gary and a frog is in the pond as well. The frog sits on the lilypad all day long and catches insects.
>
> Mark
>
> Jamee-Ann Leese 8

I LiKe PLaYiNG

iN tHa dNG

AdaM RF

Alexanderiaylonl ikePLaYINGWIth theCarSatschool

CLaSSRF

I like playing with the cars at school

Christopher Lindop RF Class

During the holiday I went to Katie Hikok's house. We played with Barney, the dog or the puppy. We went to Stone and got some sweets and a magazine. Barney is a cocker spaniel. He is very sweet. On Easter Sunday my Auntie Jenny and her two daughters, Joanna, and Alex. We call them Jo-Jo or Jo and Aly, visited us. They came from Crewe. We bought Jo and Aly a mini Barbie egg each. Jenny got me a dairy milk egg, David, a crunchie egg and Lucy a caramel egg. They were yummy. Afterwards we went on a walk down in the Nature Reserve. Then we had a small walk by the river. Jo and Aly love our cats. We have got four cats, their names our, Roddy he's ginger, Jazzy, she's black, Misty, she's grey and other colours, and Olly, he's a mixture of colours. Samantha Andrews age 8.

I wish

I wish I had a lot of friends that would play with me every day when I wanted them to. They would play the games that I wanted to play. They would be my proper friends that would help me when ever I needed help. They would be there for me and I will be there for them.

by Owen Leach age 10

I like going swimming and I like playing with the balls on the grass I like doing jobs for Mrs Hughes

Emily Thornhill   Class RH

I would like to be a world famous goal keeper when I grow up and play at Wembly for England. David Bate

Special times

My name is Rebecca Lewis but I prefer Becky. I am going to tell you two special times that I have had. The first special time for me was when my brother was born he was the cutest baby with the blondest hair I had ever seen. We ended up calling him Joseph. I used to hold him in my arm and cuddle him for hours. The second one is when I had my first puppy dog she was so soft. I used to play with her. She is a golden retriever and her name is Bonnie.

by Becky Lewis
Age 9

Freddy Thomas Classrh
i like playing with
Hannah in
the playground

when I grow up I would like to be a tennis player because its a sport

Jack Hyatt

Myself

I have orange curly hair, freckles and blue eyes. I am 9 years old. I am a jolly and good tempered person. I am shy and get embarrassed easily. I don't like to speak to alot of people out loud. I like sewing, reading and playing the flute. I can get very nervous and I don't like getting angry, although my brothers sometimes make me cross. I go to The Lonsdale C of E Primary School in Eccleshall. At school I like getting good marks in tests. I hope I can be a vet when I am older.

by
Marian Dudley

Joseph Lewis
Class RH
I like playing football on the grass

I want to be a goal keeper because I can get lots of money I want to play a against England.
Richard Vaughan

Felicity Scott   Class 4H

I like playing in the sand

Leanne age 8

Leaves are very sunny these days Every day I look at the leaves sometimes they are purple and sometimes they are brown and orange violet green its nice colours for leaves I think. even when it has been raining they grow bright. Sunny days are still cold and a bit warm.

When I grow up I will be a boxer because Rocky is a boxer.

Jamie Arnold.

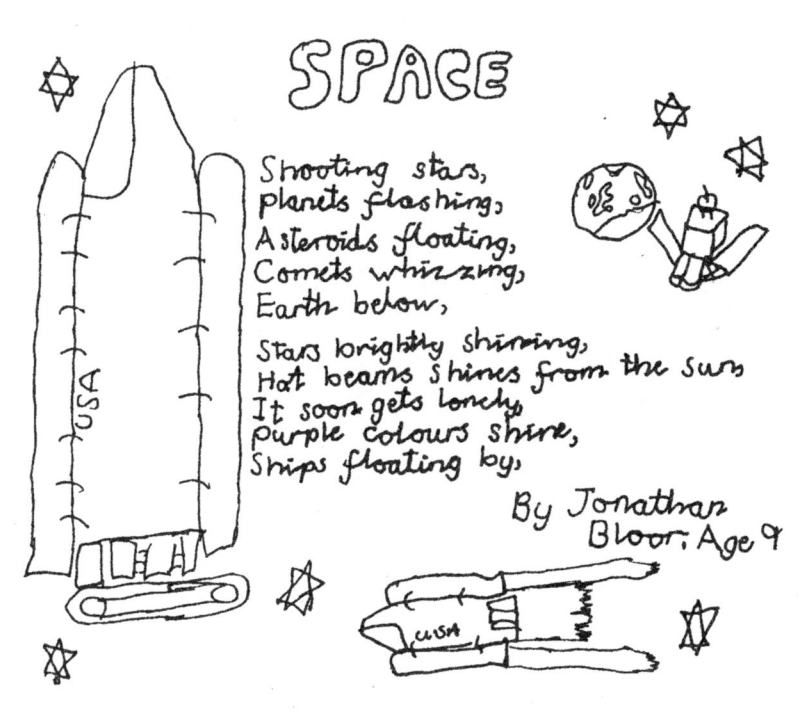

Jason's he matt
class ett
I like playing
football

SPACE

Shooting stars,
planets flashing,
Asteroids floating,
Comets whizzing,
Earth below,

Stars brightly shining,
Hot beams shines from the sun
It soon gets lonely,
Purple colours shine,
Ships floating by,

By Jonathan
Bloor, Age 9

I would like to be a tennis player be because my Daddy wished that I be a tennis player. Grace Holdcroft.

Daisywynn

I like playing at school in the shop

CLASSRF

Our environment is polluted because of oil tankers, factories and cars. When did it begin? Around fifty years ago there were fewer cars, factories or oil tankers. Sea pollution is oil and other toxins which are thrown into the sea. The R.S.P.C.A. is the Royal Society for the prevention of cruelty to animals. If oil is dumped in the sea fish, seals and even plant life is affected. Air pollution affected the ozone layer, for instance asbestos when it is burned it releases a lethal gas. Car fumes are released into the atmosphere. In march an oil tanker crashed and killed a lot of sea life. It took a long time to pull it to shore. The sea life gets less and less. The birds are affected as well because they eat the fish. The R.S.P.B look after the birds.

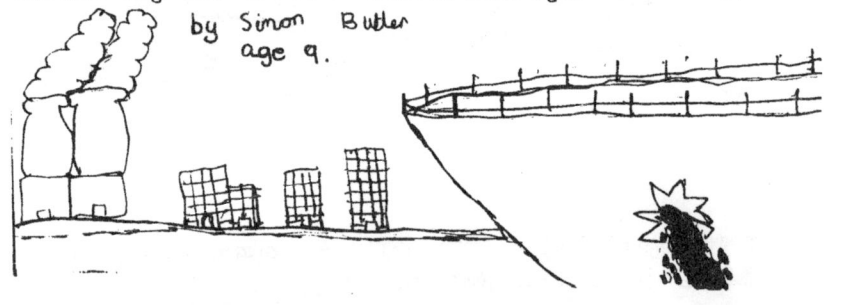

by Simon Butler
age 9.

I wish
I wish that I lived in a castle
because it would be big
I could have my own room
I wish that I had a television
in my room.
I wish I could have the biggest
room

Jessica Roestenburg 8

charlotte Stanley
I like doing
work at school

charlotte stanley
class gr

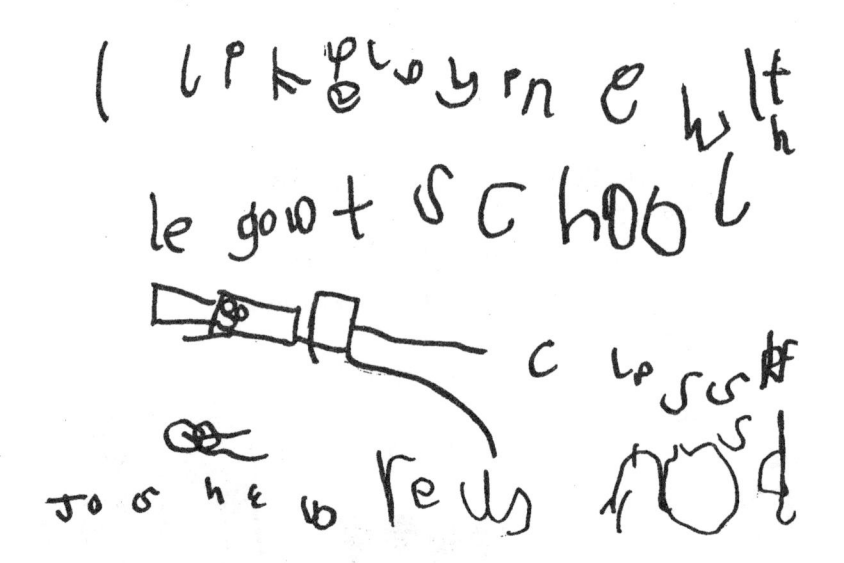

Special Times

One day at Adbaston school I was not feeling too well and was sent home. Guess what I found on the back seat of the car? A puppy which made me feel alot better. I named the puppy Bonny.
By Katie Cooke.
Age 8.

During the Easter holiday I had a game of football. After we went fishing when we got to the fishing pond the owner said that it wasn't fishing season that Saturday. I went swimming at Newport and they have put up a new black hole. That night Daniel said, "Do you want to sleep in the caravan to night, with me, Ben, Becky and Caroline who are going swimming at water world". It was fun. My name is Garry Edgar. I am nine years old.

My Self

My name is Ben Beckett. I am quite a good boy. Sometimes at home I clean my bedroom up. At school, in maths I usually finish my work quickly. I am a normal boy but a bit shy. I have got a lot of freckles and blue eyes. I am 9 years old and my best friend is StephenL. My best sport is fishing and I also like football a lot.

by Ben Beckett
Age 9

Animal friends

Pup

Kit-kat

My dog pup was 8 weeks old when we got him. He cost £40 from a farmyard. When I first got him he used to run away. I love him because HE'S MINE!. I used to run him around in the garden whilst he was a puppy and take him for long walks whilst he got bigger. My cat was 5 weeks old when we got her we called her kit-kat because she looks like chocolate. Only a few weeks ago my cat nearly died because she had an abscess on her throat. I used to call my cat a dirty Rascal because she always went in the mud and I have to clean her.

By Natalie Elliott; age 9

Ball
bowl PUP   lead

Colar
wool   Bowl

★Animal Friend★

My puppy Toby was four months old when we got him from the dogs home. He was there because he was kicked and taken out in a car and dumped on the street because he wasn't wanted. He was a christmas puppy. He didn't like men wearing black shoes when he was little. But now he's dads dog, dads his favourite. He's quite happy now he's in a good home. He enjoys eating my teddy bears and sleeping on my bean bag. I take him for a long walk every Tuesday when I come home from school. He gets a really long walk on Sundays. He's a real big RASCAL. He's my best friend. by Victoria Featherstone age 10.

Lead
Toby Bowl
Coller
Toby's favourite thing BONE!!

10TH May.

A Special time.

A special time for me was when I became an aunty. I saw my nephew when he was a few hours old. He was lying asleep in a clear plastic cot in hospital. We took a photograph of him. His name is Klye, his birthday is the 11th August 1995. He is really cute. Klye always puts his hand up by his ear and my Dad says he's on the phone. by

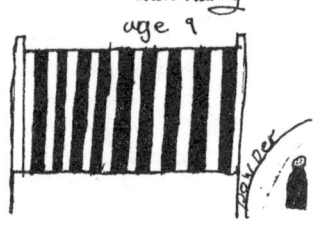

Gail Hardy age 9

Red

Red is blood.
Red is rose.
Red is dawn.
Red is red wine.
Red is a tulip.
Red is a tomato.

William Spence.

My Pirate

My Pirate has curly ginger hair at the front and spiky hair at the back. He has tiny ears. My Pirate has pink eyebrows. He has got a spotty eye and an glass eye. He has got a flat dirty nose. My Pirate has got 60 teeth made of Gold with Slobber on them. He has got a pink beard with snot in it. He's short and plumpy. He is wearing a ballet dress with a pink bow. My Pirate has no arms a fat Leg to his Knee, a wooden leg, swords coming out where his arms were. Matthew Palmer
age 8

When I grow up.

When I grow up I want to be a nurse so I can care for people and make them better. I would see if they were comfortable and take their temperature and see if they are alright. I like helping my nanny.

Victoria Abel Age 8
3 4 5

When I grow up I want to be a story teller because I like to read books. and I want to write stories for people.

Natalie Hilton

Red

Red is for rose
Red is for blood
Red is for flowers.
Red is for a red love heart

Rebecca Walker

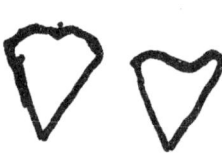

Green

Green is our uniform,
Green is grass,
Green is bouncing grasshoppers on the bouncy lawn,
Green trees taking birth on the lovely summer turf

James Fidgett

The take off.

Ten, nine, eight, seven, six
Are you ready to see Mars
and the sun. We are going to
the stars soon. The moon and
the sun. Two, one, zero! We
are taking off.

By Amy Stevens
Age 8

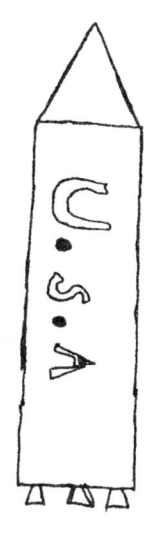

I wish to be a footballer and win the gold cup and go home with it and play football every day I wood play foot ball everyday

Robert Foxley

Red

A red apple,
A red heart,
A red flower,
A red rose,
Red blood

Kate Barraclough

My Pirate

My pirates hair is sticking out with green and pink My pirates ear are big and poking up with flees around them My pirates eye brows are long slichy and green my pirates eyes are have got green and black in and the outher has got a eye patch My Pirates nose is snotty with long hair growing out My pirates face has got a moustache with blackcurrant juice on it My Pirates shape is fat and floppy

My pirate →

Round And Round

The sun is round
A button is round
Oscar is round
A football is round
An eye is round

Jade Shaw

I wish....

I wish to be a lorrydriver because my Daddy is a lorrydriver. And because my Grandad and I sleep in the lorry. There is a topbunk.

Leslie Swinnerton

The earth goes round.
The earth goes round and round.
It turns and turns like a ball.
have you been to Space?
The Earth is a round place
It just goes round and round

Jane Bratton

What is a Book?

A book is a journey way out in space,
A book makes you red in the face,
A book is a passage way to another land,
A book can tell you about any kind of band,
A book can tell you anything!
Open a book and you will find,
Characters you left behind,
A book is a book but not an ordinary book,
It's full of magic and fun,
Books are exciting, books are delighting,
you'll find a surprise in every one.

Richard Edwards
age 10

I wish........

I wish I had a £100 so I can buy Lego. I could make a big Lego model.

Darius Satongar

I would be a policeman when I grow up so I can arrest people
Alexander Freshwater

I have got a pet rabbit. She is grey and white her name is Samantha. Every morning I go out to her cage and put some food in her bowl. I put it in the cage and she just tips it upside down. I give her a drink of cold water aswell. Sometimes I play with her. I lift the hatch and stroke her she is soft. We put Samantha in the run when it is sunny.

Kate Hughes 9

Tyson.

I have a big brown boxer dog.
Angrily he chases after me.
When he sees my friends
he barks very loudly.
My dog is half the size of me.
When I take him for a walk he jumps up and down
Runs very fast around the fields.
He gets excited jumps up at me.
Sometimes does what I say but
he scratches the wood on the door
When he wants to go out.
So we get his chain and take him.
We all ways do what he says!

by melissa
Houlton age 11

I Wish

I wish I could be seventeen
and I could take my driving test.
I also wish that when I grow up
I can be a car designer for BMW
and have a BMW 8401. I wish
this because I love cars and I
would like to be designing them
on a p.c, because I am really good
on computers and I like them a lot.
by
Dean.
Lancaster
Aged 9.

Autumn

Breezy wind.
Emerald leaves.
Rose red.
Ruby berries.
In the tree is brown.
Every leaf is changing.
Scarlet leaves.

David Timmis
Age 7

Rebecca o'kane

When I grow up I would like to be a strawbery picker and I'd like to be a strawbery picker because I like strawberries and when I go to strawberry land I pick lots of strawberries and I like strawberries when I go to strawberry land and I pick lots of them because I love picking my strawberries and I love them so much that I could hug them.

When I grow up

When I grow up I want to be an International football player for manchester utd. I would like to be a goal keeper. Oneday I wish to play in the world cup. I would not let a single goal past me.

James Bettoley

Why I like School

I like school because of playtime, because you can play with your friends and I like number work and I like reading books and I like playing with the activities and I like my teacher and I like my class room and I like p.e. and I swimming but we dont go any more and I like doing my news.

by Luke Brindley IJ

Miss Jones teaching us a lesson

My hobbies

My hobbies are Gymnastics, ballet and riding my bike. I like playing in our play house. I also like to play off ground tig. I enjoy playing the Piano and recorder. I like to play hopscotch at School. I like playing on swings, slides and see-saws. At school I like writing and drawing.

Jennifer Davies
Age 8